MORAL CAPTALISM

The Critical Examination of the Concept of Rightness
in the Context of Human Goodness

CHARLES MWEWA

DEDICATION

For my girls,
that you may constantly expend your moral capital
for the good of all humankind.

CONTENTS

DEDICATION...iii

CONTENTS..v

BRIEF INTRODUCTION ix

1 | INVESTING IN ONE'S GOOD FOR THE GOOD OF OTHERS.. 1

ICE Tenet One 1

Sources of Investing... 2

Parental Guidance.. 2

Social Mores... 2

Religious Instructions.. 3

Chastity of Conscience 3

The Concept of Locked-in-Innocence 4

Confession.. 6

Thoughts and Acts of Charity............................ 6

Value-Added Morality (VAM) 6

Conclusion 7

2 | CONTINUING TO BE GOOD TO THE POINT OF UNDUE HARDSHIPS 9

ICE Tenet Two 9

Undue Hardship 10

Social Goodness 11

Assumptions of Social Goodness 12

Inviolable Morality (In-Mo) 13

Moral Imperative 14

Right's Governing Principle 15

Conclusion 17

3 | ENDING CONDITIONS 19

ICE Tenet Three 19

Full Payment 19

    Charity Measurement 20

    Never-ending Debt Principle 20

    Consumption of Evil Bankruptcy 21

Death 21

    Death Factor #1: Love Exchange 21

    Death Factor #2: Right Exchange 22

    Death Factor #3: Restoration of Innocence 22

Conclusion 23

ABOUT THE AUTHOR 25

SELECTED BOOKS BY THIS AUTHOR 27

INDEX 33

Moral Captalism (as opposed to 'Moral *Capitalism*') may be defined by the tenets that underpin it, under the acronym of ICE: *I*nvesting in one's good for the good of others; *C*ontinuing to be good to the point of undue hardships; *E*nding only when two conditions of full payment and death have been met.

Capitalism is an economic system; Moral Captalism is a social construct. Just like in Capitalism, there is private ownership of the means of production, in Moral Captalism, individuals concerned may determine how they expend their moral capital, their moral rightness, ending in the operation of goodness for it, which is moral capital. Goodness is moral capital; *rightness* is moral profit. Individuals, thus, compete under Moral Captalism, except that they compete in outdoing each other in goodness.

They live their lives accumulating moral capital, and voluntarily expending it for others by their labor of love, and a recognition that what they own is of trust and may be used for altruistic and selfless endearments for others' benevolence.

Moral Captalism is a revolution in the *thinking-right* and *doing-right* movement. The more moral capital one has and desires to expend, the better the current state of humanity, and the more blissful the world of tomorrow.

1 | INVESTING IN ONE'S GOOD FOR THE GOOD OF OTHERS

ICE Tenet One

The first ICE tenet is subsumed into a capsule of goodness called *rightness*. To seek to be, to do and to act right, underpins Moral Captalism. The word investing in this regard means a conscious process of becoming good, first to oneself and to the end of serving others in goodness. Moral Captalism challenges itself to live a selfless life that avoids deliberate offending of others and seeks to be good to others till death.

Sources of Investing

There may be more than five sources of investing in *rightness*. The four identified in this book are: Parental guidance; social mores; religious instructions; and the Chastity of Conscience.

Parental Guidance

From birth, humans are privileged with the guidance of parents or guardians. There is placed in nature a tendency to be and to behave good to children. This intrinsic human perchance to be good to the new born is called *Infantile Moral Consciousness*. It is available in nature and does not need education or learning; it is innate in all creatures, including animals, plants, reptiles, and birds. Parents have the affinity to guide their young ones in righteousness.

Social Mores

Social mores are normative necessities available in all civilized societies. They are social standards and rules that are widely observed within a particular society or culture. They are based on the moral goodness principle. They aim to establish society on the path of righteous-ness.

Religious Instructions

In every society, there is a form of religion that exits to transmit acceptable morality in the life of the adherents. Religion is the primary source of moral attitudes and behavior in many civilized societies. Religion instructs in goodness, kindness, amity, the value of human life, acceptable social and spiritual behavior, etc. There is a presumption of *rightness* in many religions of the world.

Chastity of Conscience

Humans are born with a facility called the *Chastity of Conscience.* This facility has three compartments: Order, moral judgment and innocence. This trichotomy of social chastity is only corrupted within the environment in which a person is exposed. Humans, from infancy, seek to abide by order, to make sound moral judgments, and to preserve their innocence.

A good example is girls. Girls are not taught to protect their virginity by teachers or by social gurus; they simply know. Even without parental guidance, a girl will know that the preservation of virginity until permitted by rites to break it, is a good thing.

Boys and girls will seek to maintain a moral order, make right moral judgment, and preserve their innocence unless social influences dictate otherwise. This is true to the core of human social behavior. Indeed, humans are born with a fallen nature, but humans will never know that they had a fallen nature except by the *Chastity of Conscience* facility. This facility is at odds with the fallen nature. Humans know very early that their desire to live right, to be right and to do right is fought against by the prescriptions of the fallen nature.

The Concept of Locked-in-Innocence

The morally-inclined Concept of Locked-in-Innocence emanates from the *Chastity of Conscience*. It is rested on the idea of Thrown-Key Perception (or TKP). TKP is the natural fact of life that ensures that once innocence is locked-in, it remains so unless violated by willful actions.

TKP is responsible for the destiny of still-born and children before they reach the age of reason. TKP protects innocence. A girl will remain a virgin unless she decides to violate or give it away deliberately. Those who are raped, are still innocent because it was not the act of their will or intent. They may feel guilty or even disharmony, but they remain innocent under the theory of nature. This is because they had no intention of violating their innocence.

Innocence Maintenance is the actuality of life process. Humans live to maintain their state of innocence from the womb to the tomb. Even those who may be labeled as social deviants, misfits or worse, attempt to revert to their original state of innocence by changing behavior, prayer, confession, restitution, volunteering or other techniques. The offence that troubles their conscience is ever strong in life, even before people are exposed to religious or other moral inclinations.

There are three varieties of the *Innocence Maintenance* conception: Confession; thoughts and acts of charity; and Value-Added Morality:

Confession

The first variety of *Innocence Maintenance* is through confession. To confess is to admit, to acknowledge that one's thoughts or actions have violated one or some aspects of innocence. This acknowledgement is essential to the preservation of innocence. Those who disregard this acknowledgement may forfeit the plight of innocence.

Thoughts and Acts of Charity

To be preoccupied with thoughts and acts of charity is a noble human social responsibility, because it sustains a sense of innocence. Those who constantly live with thoughts of charity, and those who do acts of charity (love) will never be wrong in the innocence quest. It is, thus, important that humans make love their major driving force for social interactivity and survival.

Value-Added Morality (VAM)

In economics, the concept of value-added means the amount by which the value of an article is increased at each stage of its production, exclusive of initial costs. The same with morality. Initial morality is only a catalyst, at each stage of life, humans must increase their social value through many initiatives, including being right, saying right, doing right, through collaboration, cooperation, or comraderies, by helping others, volunteering, and by the Golden Rule – doing to others what they want others to do to or for them.

Conclusion

This chapter has discussed the first tenet of Moral Captalism. It has highlighted the necessity of being and doing good. Being and doing good in the context of *rightness* is social capital. In the next chapter, we discuss the second tenet, namely, that we must continue to be and do good in the context of *rightness* until we reach, in principle, the point of undue hardship.

2 | CONTINUING TO BE GOOD TO THE POINT OF UNDUE HARDSHIP

ICE Tenet Two

In the previous chapter, we discussed the first tenet of Moral Captalism. We highlighted its definition, source, and underlying principles. In this chapter, we examine the concept of undue hardship as it relates to Moral Captalism. We define and situate the concept of moral goodness and the assumptions that undergird it. And we explore both the inviolability and imperativeness of social goodness under the ambit of *rightness.*

Undue Hardship

In moral terms, undue hardship is a cut-off point, referring to special circumstances that may partially or fully exempt a person from performing a social obligation (what we may call a 'Social Good') because doing so may be overtly unreasonable or a disproportionate burden. Undue hardship is a significantly difficult or expensive action. It is a moral reason justifying the inability to do a Social Good due to its costly or healthy impact on the person called up to perform a Social Good.

A Social Good may be an action, a policy, a practice, an operation, an accommodation factor, or a service that fundamentally alters the nature or operation of a person's lifestyle, wellbeing or health if carried out under normal circumstances.

In business (or employment), an undue hardship may prevent the business from enforcing a policy or practice. In human social terms, an undue hardship may only temporarily prevent a person from performing a Social Good till one of the two conditions is met – performance is fulfilled or a person doing the action dies (or the person receiving the action dies). This last statement is the subject of discussion in Chapter 3.

Social Goodness

The idea of social goodness was first introduced in the Bible by Jesus Christ in what is known as the Social Gospel:

> When the Son of Man comes in his glory, and all the angels with him, he will sit on his throne in heavenly glory. All the nations will be gathered before him, and he will separate the people one from another as a shepherd separates the sheep from the goats. He will put the sheep on his right and the goats on his left.
>
> Then the King will say to those on his right, 'Come, you who are blessed by my Father; take your inheritance, the kingdom prepared for you since the creation of the world. *For I was hungry and you gave me something to eat, I was thirsty and you gave me something to drink, I was a stranger and you invited me in, I needed clothes and you clothed me, I was sick and you looked after me, I was in prison and you came to visit me.*'
>
> Then the righteous will answer him, 'Lord, when did we see you hungry and feed you, or thirsty and give you something to drink? When did we see you a stranger and invite you in, or needing clothes and clothe you? When did we see you sick or in prison and go to visit

you?'

The King will reply, 'I tell you the truth, whatever you did for one of the least of these brothers of mine, you did for me.'[1]

Assumptions of Social Goodness

Moral Captalism assumes the following. First, it assumes that there are social *needs*. These needs have been summarized in the Social Gospel passage (also known as the *Mathew 25 Dialogue*) as: Hunger, thirsty, accommodation, lack of clothing, poor health, imprisonment and security issues (such as lack of comfort or safety).

Second, Moral Captalism assumes that these needs are *prevalent* in society. This assumption means that there is need everywhere, and that everyone has an opportunity to help someone in need.

Third, it assumes that prevailing needs can be found in, or have to do with, the *least* among the people. In other words, the people who are likely to have these needs are the poor, the marginalized and the helpless.

Fourth, it assumes that everyone who has the capabilities must *be aware* of the social needs

---

[1] Mathew 25:31-40 (New International Version – NIV)

around them and should *meet* them or some of them.

And fifth, it assumes that social needs are *context-specific*. Thus, one may not only receive social help but must also give social help. For example, a poor person may receive food and drink, but they should be able to visit those in prison or share accommodation with strangers, etc.

A poor country may receive monetary donations from a rich country, but it should be able to accommodate the unspiritual or unmoral needs of the rich country. A rich country may have the capacity to cure poverty but it may lack the capacity to deal with greed, etc. Therefore, everyone and every nation must have the opportunity to perform a Moral Good. There are no exceptions.

Inviolable Morality (In-Mo)

There is no ending to the provision of moral goodness. The idea of undue hardship, by implication, suggests that there is, in practice, no place where one might think that not being good or doing good is justifiable. This is the basis of *In-Mo*. Not doing good is a nullity.

In-Mo is the underlying principle giving impetus to punitive legislations and regulatory coding. In legal or political parlance, *In-Mo* is coded and is enforceable by courts of law. However, in the social context, Moral Good is an individual choice.

In Moral Captalism, there are official or legislated or legally enforceable requirements to be good. However, there is a *Law of Conscience* that dictates that all evil is punishable. That punishment may happen within life or after death. For example, in major religions, punishment for immorality happens after Judgment Day. Socially, many societies believe that nature punishes wrong doings, and such manifestations may range from sickness, to bad luck, to banishing, to losing favor, or to premature death, etc.

Moral Imperative

This is book is titled 'Moral *Captalism*,' and not 'Moral Capitalism." This is because the idea of morality is a supreme thesis embedded in natural law. However, the sensibilities of Moral Captalism have a social-monetary construct. Thus, the imperative rests on morality as a capital (asset) of goodness.

In-Mo is a veracity of moral imperative. Even in uncivilized or excessively uncivil societies where they do not respect human dignity, there is always some notion of justice (morality, or a sense of right and wrong). People understand that bad actions must lead to some form of punitive response. This is a moral imperative. Thus, whether one does Moral Good for themselves or for others, the imperative of morality takes precedence. Morality is capital.

In short, humans are condemned to doing good, and must do good, all the days of their lives. Any divergence must receive some form of penalty, in one way or the other. Bad behavior, deviancy, crime, or delinquency are, therefore, socially unacceptable or unjustifiable.

Right's Governing Principle

Moral goodness cannot be achieved without a governing principle of *rightness* imbedded in nature (natural law). Thus, humans may, philosophically, debate whether right and wrong exist or are contextual, and even idiosyncratic, but natural law overrides. Right is always right.

Goodness is presumed to be right, and right is always good, no matter how it manifests.

Thus, right may be realized through difficulty, challenges or even death. In religion, for example, God required Job to pass through an untold calamitous experience, losing his wealth and family and suffering from sore boils, but right was justified. In other words, his experience was not good, but it was right.

God required His Son, Jesus Christ, to suffer pain and death on the Cross. The experience was bad, but the expression was right. Freedom fighters, war veterans and soldiers may die (bad) in the process of fighting for their rights, but their actions may still be right.

In Moral Captalism, the end does not justify the means. What is germane is intent. The intent must be founded in *rightness*, even if the process may seem wrong or bad. Thus, the road to bliss may pass through hell as long as the end is heaven. That should be justified under Moral Captalism.

A good social example is where a parent requires his children to do extreme menial work (which may not be good in the interim), but it is right – children would benefit from the final outcome. Bitter medicine may not be good, but it is right. Parental discipline may be bad, but it is right, etc.

It is important, though, to delineate Moral Captalism from the Machiavellian thesis of ends justifying the means. Under Moral Captalism, we do not do bad to others so that good may result. We do not seek to harm others because it could benefit them, either. Rather, Moral Captalism is a judicious and moral imperative. Its ethos lies in good intentionality, leading to moral goodness, to the end that right may be done. The process must be *moral* as the results are *right*. In stating this, we do not contract bad experiences that lead to a good end, as long as the intent was good.

Conclusion

This chapter has discussed the second tenet of Moral Captalism. It requires one to be good in the interest of *rightness* to the point where it becomes unattainable. In principle, that is a given. However, in practice, being and doing good may not be subject to undue hardship. In the next chapter, we discuss the conditions that may, in principle, offset the undue hardship requirement.

3 | ENDING CONDITIONS

ICE Tenet Three

Social capital is contained in the idea of being socially good to the point of undue hardship, or to the point where we either expend our social capital to the fullest or we die attempting to do so. This is the subject of the present chapter.

Full Payment

We expend our social capital to the fullest when one of the three things have happened. These are through Charity Measurement; the Never-ending Debt Principle; and Consumption of Evil Bankruptcy.

Charity Measurement

Works of charity or works of love are the quintessential and the best form of consummation of one's moral capital. Works of charity are diverse and are encapsulated in the *Mathew 25 Dialogue*, discussed in Chapter 2.

Never-ending Debt Principle

This is akin to Charity of Measurement but it is realized in smaller, even mundane, deeds of love. A Christian philosopher put it this way, "Let no debt remain outstanding, except the continuing debt to love one another, for whoever loves others has fulfilled the law."[2] There is no prison, no incarceration that can hold someone who practices love. Each day, one must remember to repay the debt of love to all those who are around them or who they come across.

---

[2] Romans 13:8

Consumption of Evil Bankruptcy

One has fulfilled or consummated their full payment when they become evilly bankrupt. In other works, they cannot do or be evil anymore. It is a high threshold to reach except by special grace. It must be worked towards though it may be impossible to attain. Working towards it itself is necessary to its consumption.

Death

Death by itself is not a bequeathal of moral expenditures. Only love that is either encountered in the process of meeting one of the three elements of full payment (discussed above) or meets one of the three components of the death factor discussed below. The death factors are: Love Exchange; Right Exchange; and *Restoration of Innocence*.

Death Factor #1: Love Exchange

To have fully expended one's moral capital and to remain within a state of morally inviolability, one must have exchanged their love for death in death. In short, a death that comes within the realm of being loving and doing works of love is a welcome death – because it subscribes in full to the underpinned conception of Moral Captalism. People must only seek to die after or while being loving or doing works of love.

Death Factor #2: Right Exchange

Like with Love Exchange, one must seek to die within the context of *rightness*. Death has no teeth against those who either died loving or died while being right.

Death Factor #3: Restoration of Innocence

Restoration of Innocence is a deliberate undertaking to relieve oneself of works of the flesh or carnal machinations. To put it differently, the *Restoration of Innocence* is the return to pre-seven-year-old innocence. It can be achieved through remorsity (the state of being remorseful), confession (admitting one's anti-social, evil nature and actions) and restitution (or admission of wrong and compensating for such admissions).

Conclusion

This chapter has discussed the last tenet of Moral Captalism. In summary, Moral Captalism rests on three tenets, that one must invest in good for the good of others; one must continue to be good to the point of undue hardship; and one must consummate or expend their moral capital up to full payment or through death that meets one or more elements of full payment or death. ICE is the acronym for the three tenets. ICE is enshrined under the principle of *rightness*.

ABOUT THE AUTHOR

Award-Winning, Best-Selling Author, Charles Mwewa
(LLB; BA Law; BA Ed; LLM), is a prolific researcher, poet,
novelist, lawyer, law professor and Christian apologist and
intercessor. Mwewa has written no less than 100 books and
counting in every genre and has exhibited his works at
prestigious expos like the Ottawa International Book Expo
and is the winner of the Coppa Awards for his signature
publication, *Zambia: Struggles of My People*.
Mwewa and his family live in the Canadian Capital City of
Ottawa.

SELECTED BOOKS BY THIS AUTHOR

1. *ZAMBIA: Struggles of My People (First and Second Editions)*
2. *10 FINANCIAL & WEALTH ATTITUDES TO AVOID*
3. *10 STRATEGIES TO DEFEAT STRESS AND DEPRESSION: Creating an Internal Safeguard against Stress and Depression*
4. *100+ REASONS TO READ BOOKS*
5. *A CASE FOR AFRICA?S LIBERTY: The Synergistic Transformation of Africa and the West into First-World Partnerships*
6. *A PANDEMIC POETRY, COVID-19*
7. *ALLERGIC TO CORRUPTION: The Legacy of President Michael Sata of Zambia*
8. *BOOK ABOUT SOMETHING: On Ultimate Purpose*
9. *CAMPAIGN FOR AFRICA: A Provocative Crusade for the Economic and Humanitarian Decolonization of Africa*
10. *CHAMPIONS: Application of Common Sense and Biblical Motifs to Succeed in Both Worlds*
11. *CORONAVIRUS PRAYERS*
12. *HH IS THE RIGHT MAN FOR ZAMBIA: And Other Acclaimed Articles on Zambia and Africa*
13. *I BOW: 3500 Prayer Lines of Inspiration & Intercession from the Heart: Volume One*
14. *INTERUNIVERSALISM IN A NUTSHELL: For Iranian Refugee Claimants*
15. *LAW & GRACE: An Expository Study in the Rudiments of Sin and Truth*
16. *LAWS OF INFLUENCE: 7even Lessons in Transformational Leadership*
17. *LOVE IDEAS IN COVID PANDEMIC TIMES:*

For Couples & Lovers

18. *P.A.S.S: Version 2: Answer Bank*
19. *P.A.S.S.: Acing the Ontario Paralegal-Licensing Examination, Version 2*
20. *POETRY: The Best of Charles Mwewa*
21. *QUOT-EBOS: Essential. Barbs. Opinions. Sayings*
22. *REASONING WITH GOD IN PRAYER: Poetic Verses for Peace & Unconfronted Controversies*
23. *RESURRECTION: (A Spy in Hell Novel)*
24. *I DREAM OF AFRICA: Poetry of Post-Independence Africa, the Case of Zambia*
25. *SERMONS: Application of Legal Principles and Procedures in the Life and Ministry of Christ*
26. *SONG OF AN ALIEN: Over 130 Poems of Love, Romance, Passion, Politics, and Life in its Complexity*
27. *TEMPORARY RESIDENCE APPLICATION*
28. *THE GRACE DEVOTIONAL: Fifty-two Happy Weeks with God*
29. *THE SYSTEM: How Society Defines & Confines Us: A Worksheet*
30. *FAIRER THAN GRACE: My Deepest for His Highest*
31. *WEALTH THINKING: And the Concept of Capisolism*
32. *PRAYER: All Prayer Makes All Things Possible*
33. *PRAYER: All Prayer Makes All Things Possible, Answers*
34. *PRISONER OF GRACE: An I Saw Jesus at Milton Vision*
35. *PRAYERS OF OUR CHILDREN*
36. *TEN BASIC LESSONS IN PRAYER*
37. *VALLEY OF ROSES: City Called Beautiful*
38. *THE PATCH THEOREM: A Philosophy of Death, Life and Time*
39. *50 RULES OF POLITICS: A Rule Guide on Politics*
40. *ALLERGIC TO CORRUPTION: The Legacy of*

President Michael Sata of Zambia

41. *INTRODUCTION TO ZAMBIAN ENVIRONMENTAL LEGISLATIVE SCHEME*

42. *REFUGEE PROTECTION IN CANADA: For Iranian Christian Convert Claimants*

43. *LAW & POVERTY (unpublished manuscript)*

44. *CHRISTIAN CONTROVERSIES: Loving Homosexuals*

45. *THINKING GOVERNMENT: Principles & Predilections*

46. *WHY MARRIED COUPLES LIE TO EACH OTHER: A Treatise*

47. *LOVE & FRIENDSHIP TIPS FOR GEN Z*

48. *POVERTY DISCOURSE: Spiritual Imperative or Social Construct*

49. *SEX BEFORE WEDDING: The Tricky Trilemma*

50. *QUOTABLE QUOTES EXCELLENCE, VOL. 1: Knowledge & Secrets*

51. *QUOTABLE QUOTES EXCELLENCE, VOL. 2: Love & Relationships*

52. *QUOTABLE QUOTES EXCELLENCE, VOL. 3: Hope*

53. *QUOTABLE QUOTES EXCELLENCE, VOL. 4: Justice, Law & Morality*

54. *QUOTABLE QUOTES EXCELLENCE, VOL. 5: Dreams & Vision*

55. *QUOTABLE QUOTES EXCELLENCE, VOL. 6: Character & Perseverance*

56. *QUOTABLE QUOTES EXCELLENCE, VOL. 7: Actions*

57. *QUOTABLE QUOTES EXCELLENCE, 1 of 20: Knowledge & Secrets*

58. *QUOTABLE QUOTES EXCELLENCE, 2 of 20: Love & Relationships*

59. *QUOTABLE QUOTES EXCELLENCE, 3 of 20: Hope*

60. *QUOTABLE QUOTES EXCELLENCE, 4 of 20: Justice, Law & Morality*

61. *QUOTABLE QUOTES EXCELLENCE, 5 of 20: Vision & Dreams*

62. *THE SEVEN LAWS OF LOVE*

63. *THE BURDEN OF ZAMBIA*

64. *BEMBA DYNASTY I (1 of a Trilogy)*

65. *BEMBA DYNASTY II (2 of a Trilogy)*

66. *ETHICAL MENTORSHIP: Missing Link in Transformational Leadership*

67. *AFRICA MUST BE DEVELOPED: Agenda for the 22nd Century Domination*

68. *INNOVATION: The Art of Starting Something New*

69. *TOWARDS TRUE ACHIEVEMENT: The Mundane & the Authentic*

70. *ONE WORLD UNDER PRAYER: For Camerron, Ecuador, and France*

71. *ONE WORLD UNDER PRAYER: For New Zealand, Poland, and Uganda*

72. *ONE WORLD UNDER PRAYER: For Malta, USA, and Zambia*

73. *ONE WORLD UNDER PRAYER: For Germany*

74. *ONE WORLD UNDER PRAYER: For Haiti, Iraq, and Russia*

75. *ONE WORLD UNDER PRAYER: For Chad, UN, and Syria*

76. *ONE WORLD UNDER PRAYER: For Burundi, Canada, and Israel*

77. *ONE WORLD UNDER PRAYER: For China, Egypt, and Venezuela*

78. *ONE WORLD UNDER PRAYER: For Greece, Mali, and Ukraine*

79. *ONE WORLD UNDER PRAYER: For Morocco, North Korea, and the UK*

80.   *ONE WORLD UNDER PRAYER: For Belgium,*
      Brazil, and the Burkina Faso
81.   *ADIEU PERFECTIONS: A Satire*
82.   *OPTIMIZATION: Turning Low Moments into High*
      Comments
83.   *ACING THE IMPOSSIBLE: Faith in the Other*
      Dimension
84.   *END GAME LAW: Financial Mindset in Quotables*
85.   *MARRIAGE MAPPING METHODOLOGY: The*
      Outline of How to Measure the Strength, Love-Condition
      and Longevity of a Marriage
86.   *A CASE AGAINST WAR: The Imperative of Love*
      and the Unsustainability of Peace
87.   *BORROW TO GROW: Accessing Other's Achievements*
      to Your Benefit
88.   *WESTERN CHRISTIANITY NEVER BEEN*
      PURE: A Treatise
89.   *MISERABLE UNSAVING: A Poetic Satire on*
      Money Mindset for Non-Saving Upbringings
90.   *MORAL CAPTALISM: The Critical Examination of*
      the Concept of Rightness in the Context of Human Goodness

INDEX

A

accommodation, 10, 12, 13
Africa, 27, 28
Assumptions of Social Goodness, 12

B

bad luck, 14
behavior, 3, 4, 5, 15
being right. *See* VAM
benevolence, x
business, 10

C

Capitalism, ix, x, 1, 7, 9, 12, 14, 16, 17, 22, 23
Charity Measurement. *See* Full Payment
Chastity of Conscience, 2, 3
Chastity of Conscience facility, 4
children, 16
choice, 14
Christian, 25
clothing, 12
collaboration. *See* VAM
comfort, 12
comraderies. *See* VAM
Concept of Locked-in-Innocence, 4
confession. *See* Innocence Maintenance
Consumption of Evil Bankruptcy. *See* Full Payment

cooperation. *See* VAM

courts of law, 14

Cross. *See* Jesus Christ

culture, 3

D

death, ix, 1, 14, 16,
21, 23

Death, 21

delinquency. *See*
deviancy

deviancy, 15

discipline. *See*
children

doing right. *See* VAM

donations, 13

E

economics, 6

employment, 10

F

fallen nature, 4

favor, 14

full payment, ix, 21,

23

Full Payment, 19

G

God, 28

Golden Rule. *See* VAM

goodness, ix, 1, 3, 9,
11, 13, 15

guardians, 2

H

health, 10, 12, 13

helping others. *See*
VAM

helpless, 12

hunger, 12

I

ICE. *See* Moral
Capitalism

ICE Tenet One, 1

ICE Tenet Three, 19

ICE Tenet Two, 9

imperativeness, 9

Infantile Moral

Consciousness, 2
In-Mo. See Inviolable
   Morality
innocence, 3, 4, 5, 6
Innocence
   Maintenance, 5
intent, 16
intentionality, 17
inviolability, 9
Inviolable Morality, 13

J

Jesus Christ, 16
Judgment Day, 14

L

labor of love, ix
law, 25
lawyer, 25
Love Exchange, 21

M

Machiavellian thesis,
   17
marginalized, 12

Mathew 25 Dialogue.
   See Social Gospel
moral capital, iii, ix, x,
   20, 21, 23
Moral Captalism, ix, 1,
   9, 14, 16, 17, 23
moral imperative, 15

N

necessities, 2
Never-ending Debt
   Principle. *See* Full
   Payment

O

opportunity, 12, 13

P

pain. *See* Jesus Christ
parents, 2
policy, 10
poor, 12, 13
prison, 11, 13, 20
private ownership, ix
professor, 25

punishment, 14

punitive response, 15

R

Religious Instructions, 3

remorsity, 22

restitution, 22

Restoration of Innocence. *See* Death

rich country, 13

Right Exchange. *See* Death

righteous-ness, 2, 3

rightness, ix, 1, 2, 3, 7, 9, 15, 16, 17, 22, 23

S

safety, 12

saying right. *See* VAM

security, 12

sickness, 14

social deviants, 5

Social Good, 10

Social Gospel, 11, 12

social help, 13

social influences, 4

social interactivity, 6

Struggles of My People, 25, 27

T

the West, 27

thirsty, 11, 12

thoughts and acts of charity. *See* Innocence Maintenance

Thrown-Key Perception, 4

TKP. *See* Thrown-Key Perception

U

undue hardships, ix

unspiritual or unmoral needs, 13

V

Value-Added
  Morality. *See*
  Innocence
  Maintenance
VAM. *See* Value
  Added Morality
virginity, 4
volunteering. *See*

VAM

W

works of love, 20, 22
wrong, 6

Z

Zambia, 25, 27, 28, 29